Prentice Hall Regents

# MONSTERS!

PRENTICE HALL REGENTS

A VIACOM COMPANY

# Getting Ready to Read

**Can you find all the monsters?**

appear     sneak
gush     fire
breathe     destroy
gobble up     terrible
snatch     explode
flame     horrible

# THE DRAGON WHO ALMOST ATE NEW YORK CITY

## By Steven Otfinoski

One day without warning, a dragon appeared in New York City. Maybe the dragon was sleeping when workers on a new building disturbed its cave. That's what some people said.

Where the dragon came from didn't matter. He was *there* now and that was the problem.

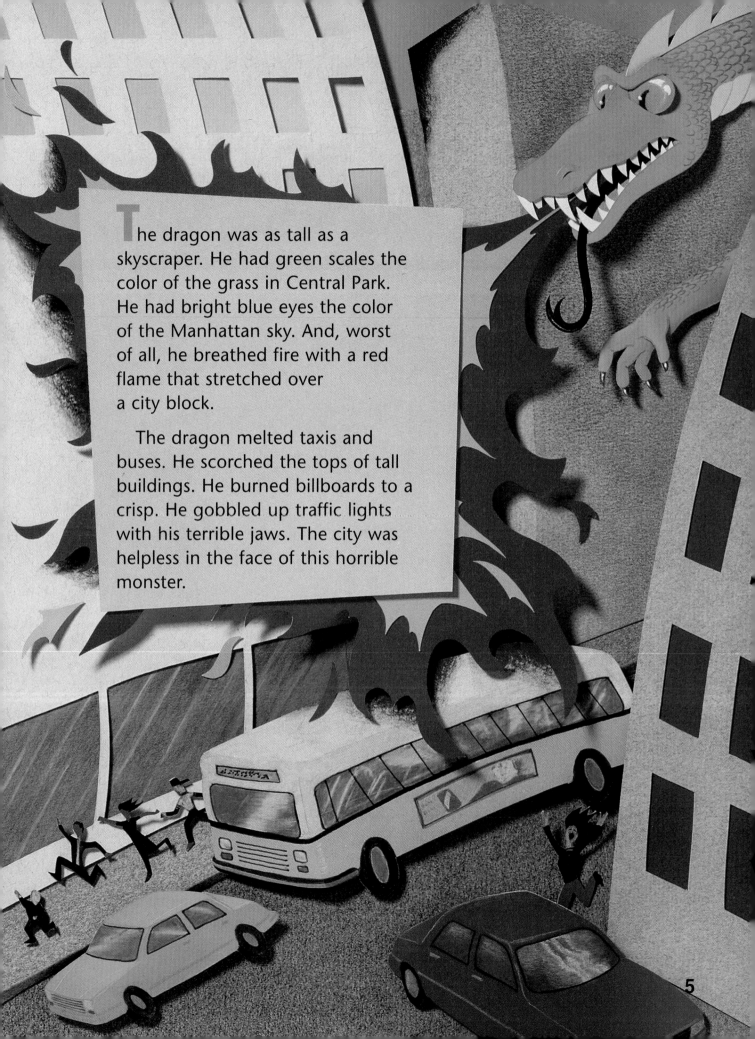

The dragon was as tall as a skyscraper. He had green scales the color of the grass in Central Park. He had bright blue eyes the color of the Manhattan sky. And, worst of all, he breathed fire with a red flame that stretched over a city block.

The dragon melted taxis and buses. He scorched the tops of tall buildings. He burned billboards to a crisp. He gobbled up traffic lights with his terrible jaws. The city was helpless in the face of this horrible monster.

A boy named Ralph was walking home from school when the dragon attacked. Ralph was brave, but he was smart, too. When he saw the destruction caused by the dragon, Ralph decided to do something. On a street corner he saw a fire hydrant and a pretzel cart whose owner was frightened away. Just then, Ralph got an idea.

When the dragon came around the corner, Ralph threw a big, soft pretzel up into the monster's open mouth.

The dragon never tasted a pretzel before that day. He found it delicious! The monster looked down and saw the pretzel cart. He stretched out a clawed foot, snatched up all the pretzels, and ate every last one.

The salt from the pretzels gave the dragon a terrible thirst. Ralph sneaked over to the fire hydrant and opened it. Water gushed out. The dragon rushed to the open hydrant and greedily drank the gushing water.

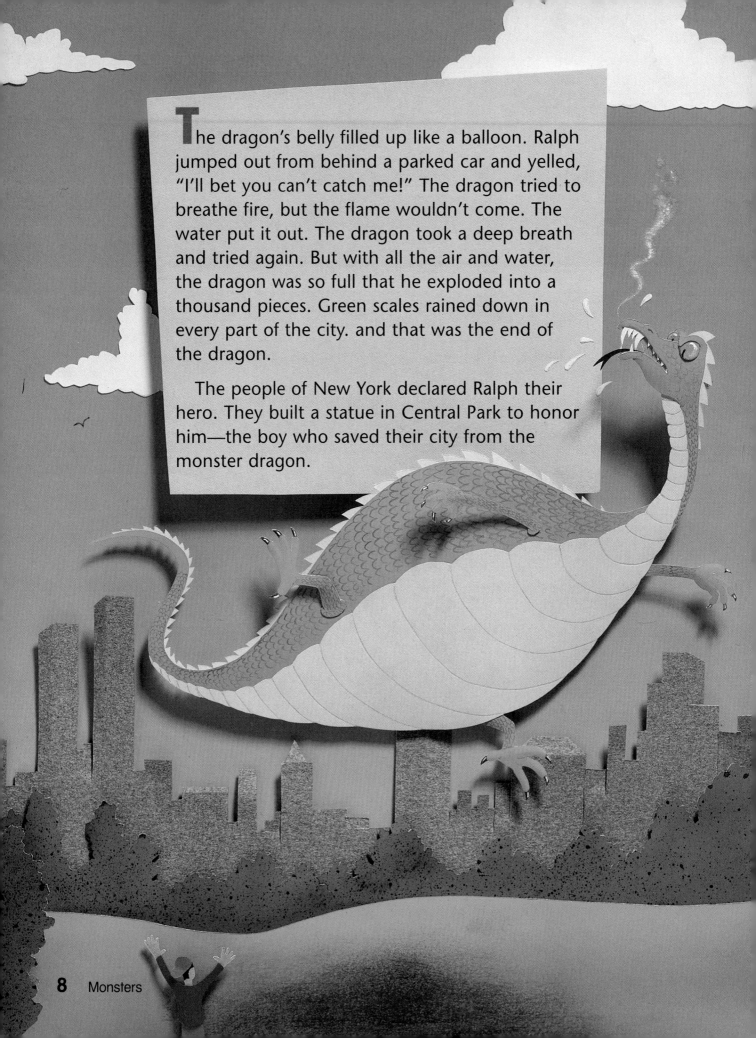

The dragon's belly filled up like a balloon. Ralph jumped out from behind a parked car and yelled, "I'll bet you can't catch me!" The dragon tried to breathe fire, but the flame wouldn't come. The water put it out. The dragon took a deep breath and tried again. But with all the air and water, the dragon was so full that he exploded into a thousand pieces. Green scales rained down in every part of the city. and that was the end of the dragon.

The people of New York declared Ralph their hero. They built a statue in Central Park to honor him—the boy who saved their city from the monster dragon.

# After You Read

What happened first? What happened next?
Use the pictures to tell the story.

# EVERYDAY TALK

## •Asking for or offering help in an emergency

Read the cartoon strip.
What emergency do you see?
Who is asking for help?
What is he saying?
Who is offering help?
What is she saying?

# Getting Ready to Read

**Read the time line. It shows many animals that have lived on Earth. Some are prehistoric and have died out.**

| | | |
|---|---|---|
| 14–26 million years ago | | Whales, birds, and bears appear. |
| 26–55 million years ago | | Monkeys, cats, dogs, and elephants appear. |
| 65 million years ago | | Last dinosaurs die. |
| 130 million years ago | | Triceratops and Ankylosaurus are common. |
| 180 million years ago | | Stegosaurus and Apatosaurus are common. |
| 225 million years ago | | Plateosaurus and Lystrosaurus are common. |
| 275 million years ago | | Snakes, fish, and frogs are common. |
| 405 million years ago | | Insects appear. |

**How long ago did the first dinosaurs live on Earth?**
**How long ago did the last ones die?**

**Look at the two kinds of reptiles. How are they alike? How are they different?**

| | | | | | |
|---|---|---|---|---|---|
| Tyrannosaurus rex 8 tons | | | | | |
| Crocodile 1/2 ton | | | | | |
| Feet | 0 | 10 | 20 | 30 | 40 |

Both animals have sharp teeth and heavy bones.

Both are meat–eaters.

Both animals hatch from eggs.

Scientists have found fossils of both animals in layers of old rock.

A full–grown Tyrannosaurus rex was much bigger than the biggest crocodile, one of the biggest reptiles alive today.

Which animal still lives on Earth? Which animal has disappeared?

11

# WHAT HAPPENED TO THE DINOSAURS?

## ◆ BY FRANKLYN M. BRANLEY ◆

What happened to the dinosaurs?

Dinosaurs lived on Earth for 140 million years. Then, 65 million years ago, they disappeared. Other reptiles disappeared, too— flying reptiles and reptiles that lived in the sea. Many other kinds of animals also died out. And many kinds of plants.

No one knows why the dinosaurs disappeared. But there are many theories. A theory is an idea. It is an explanation that might be possible.

Maybe small animals ate dinosaur eggs so only a few eggs were able to hatch. This is one theory. But this theory does not explain why other kinds of animals died out, and many plants as well.

Maybe a group of dinosaurs got sick and the sickness spread to other groups. But if that happened, chances are the sickness would not have reached reptiles that lived in the sea.

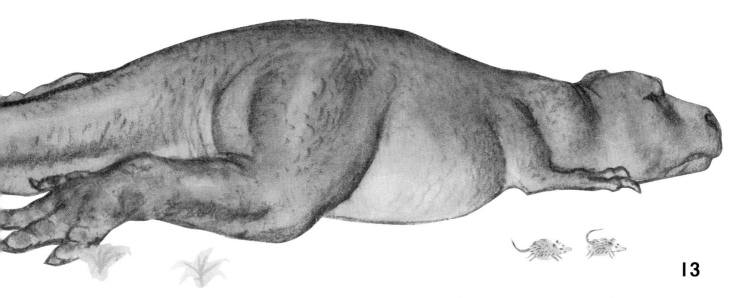

Some people have suggested that for a time the sun became cooler and did not shine as brightly. That made Earth cooler, so plants could not grow well. Some dinosaurs were meat eaters—they ate other dinosaurs. But many dinosaurs ate plants. They needed a lot of food. If Earth cooled so much the plants could not grow, plant-eating and meat-eating dinosaurs would have starved.

Another theory was suggested by scientists who were exploring old layers of rocks. In rock layers 65 million years old they found dinosaur fossils. And they found a layer of black soot, or carbon, that might have been produced by a great fire.

Sixty-five million years ago thousands of comets may have crashed into Earth. That would have produced a lot of heat. Wildfires would have swept through forests and swamps. Plants would have burned up, and dinosaurs would have, too.

After the fire had burned out, the theory says, the air was heavy with soot, ash, and dust. There was so much, the sun could not shine through. Earth got colder and colder. Many plants that had survived the fire could not grow. There was little food for any dinosaurs that might have survived the Earth fire. So they starved.

Why the dinosaurs disappeared is still a mystery.

# After You Read

**Work with a partner to make a "Dinosaur Question and Answer" game.**

**1** Write one question about dinosaurs on each of five cards.

**2** Trade cards with your partner. Write the answer to each question on the back of the card.

**3** Take your cards back. Check the answers. If they are wrong, correct them together.

**4** Put all the cards in a box to play a class quiz game. Teams take turns answering questions. Each correct answer is worth five points. The team with the highest score wins.

Things you will need:

# EVERYDAY TALK

## • Making a guess
## • Stating possibilities

I WONDER WHAT HAPPENED TO PEDRO.

I GUESS HE FORGOT.

MAYBE HE CHANGED HIS MIND.

SATURDAY SHOW TIMES 12, 2, 4

**What do you think the boy says?**

# PART 3

# Monster Time

## MONSTER WEEK ON TV

### Mon.
### After-School Cartoon Special ▶

See a monstrous collection of cartoon favorites. Includes *Dinosaur Rock*, *Mighty Rangers Against the Thing*, and *Merry Monsters from Mars*.

AFN Channel 29, 8:00 P.M.

### Tues.
### Conversations with Ricky Miranda ▶

Hear the 11-year-old star of *Slimy Stuff from Outer Space* talk about making the film: "It was really scary, but it was worth it."

PTS Channel 51, 9:00 P.M.

### Wed. ▲
### Real-Life Monsters

The focus of this week's documentary is Indonesia's Komodo dragon, the world's biggest lizard.

PTS Channel 51, 7:00 P.M..

### ◀ Thurs.
### When Monsters Roamed the Earth (1993)

A feature-length animated film set in the Jurassic period. It's a tale of conflicts among the dinosaurs. Rated G.

AFN Channel 29, 7:00 P.M.

### ◀ Fri.
### Nightmare at Swamp Manor (1978)

British horror-shocker about stranded guests attacked by monster frogs. Cardboard characters, but some truly creepy moments. Definitely not for the young or the timid. Rated PG-13.

AFN Channel 29, 10:00 P.M.

# T-Rex Uncovered in Montana

BOZEMAN, MT, Oct. 22—Scientists report finding the most complete fossil skeleton yet of a Tyrannosaurus rex. The skeleton was found with lower arm bones. Scientists hope these bones will give them clues about how Tyrannosaurus rex used its tiny arms. A team of scientists from the Museum of the Rockies in Bozeman, Montana, found the 65-million-year-old fossil skeleton. Scientists call the discovery the most important find in years.

## Monster Riddles

1. Why couldn't the dragon go to the movies?
2. What do you get when you cross a frog and a dinosaur?
3. What can leap tall buildings in a single bound and eat them in a single bite?

**Answers: 1.** Because the theater had a "no smoking" policy. **2.** A leaping lizard. **3.** Super Dragon.

# Stranger Than Fiction

The woolly mammoth, which became extinct about 10,000 years ago, was much bigger than modern-day elephants. Bodies of mammoths found preserved in ice in Siberia have been shown to reach a height of over fourteen feet.

Scientists still have doubts about the existence of Bigfoot, the 10-foot-tall apelike creature with the huge feet, which has been spotted by hundreds of people in the mountains of the Pacific Northwest.

In 1960 Tim Dinsdale filmed a monster he said was real at Loch Ness, a lake in northern Scotland. There have been many sightings of the Loch Ness monster since the first one in A.D. 565.

## •Expressing surprise or disbelief

This is what you say when you are surprised or don't believe what you see or hear.

No kidding?
Incredible!
Unbelievable!
For real?

Wow!
No way!
I don't believe it!
Amazing!

What would you say if you read these headlines? Act this out with a partner.

*SPECIAL EDITION* **NEWS** 25¢

### Men from Mars Land at the White House

A Martian spaceship landed on the White House lawn early yesterday morning. The presi-

### 10-Year-Old Wins Nobel Prize

Enrique Martínez, the 10-year-old Guatemalan writer, won the Nobel Prize for literature yesterday. His famous books about "Life in Guate-

### Schools Close Until 2005

School boards all over the country have agreed to close schools until 2005. Instead of going to school, students will

Make up your own unbelievable headlines.

HERE
AND
THERE

Legless
dragon

Ethiopian
dragon

Algonquin
dragon

Aztec
dragon

Japanese
dragon

Chinese
dragon

Describe each dragon and tell where it comes from.

# Theme Project

Are you ready to put on your play? To find out, talk with your partner or group. Use the following checklist.

**1**

☐ Our sets are ready.

**2**

☐ Our script is finished. We've read through it several times and made all the necessary changes.

**3**

☐ We have all the costumes and props we need. The prop people know when to give props to the actors.

**4**

☐ The actors have read through their parts several times.

**5**

☐ Our sound effects are ready.

**6**

☐ The actors know when to enter and exit the "stage."

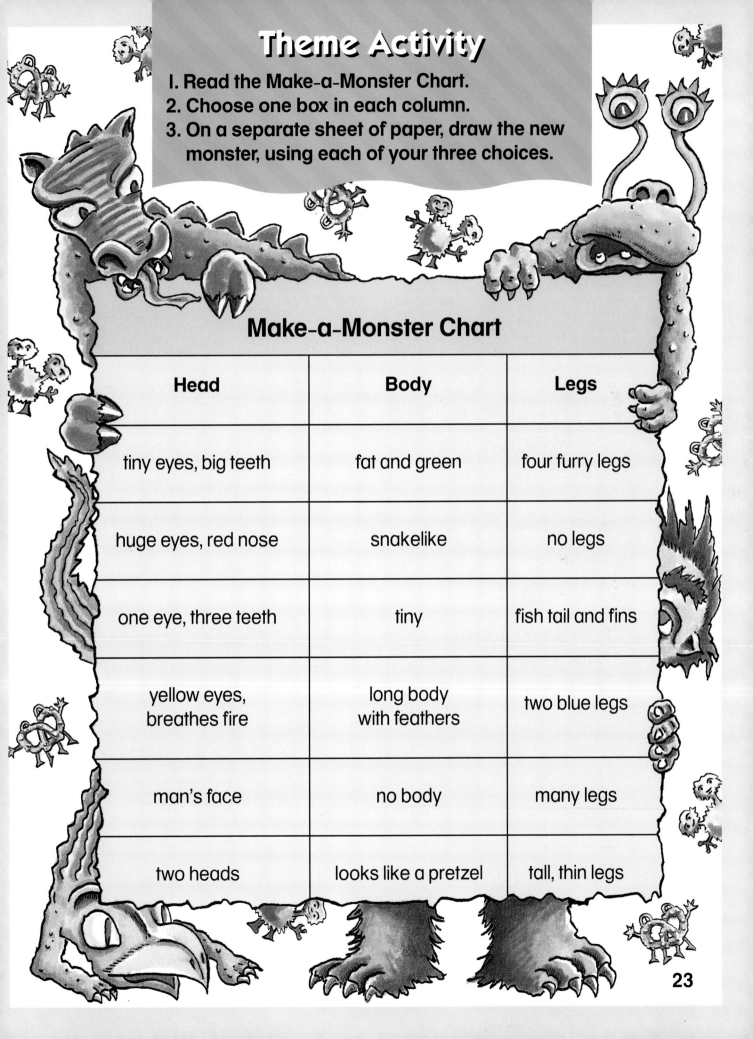

# Theme Activity

1. Read the Make-a-Monster Chart.
2. Choose one box in each column.
3. On a separate sheet of paper, draw the new monster, using each of your three choices.

## Make-a-Monster Chart

| Head | Body | Legs |
|------|------|------|
| tiny eyes, big teeth | fat and green | four furry legs |
| huge eyes, red nose | snakelike | no legs |
| one eye, three teeth | tiny | fish tail and fins |
| yellow eyes, breathes fire | long body with feathers | two blue legs |
| man's face | no body | many legs |
| two heads | looks like a pretzel | tall, thin legs |

23

**Prentice Hall Regents**
**Publisher:** Marilyn Lindgren
**Project Editors:** Carol Callahan, Kathleen Ossip
**Assistant Editor:** Susan Frankle
**Director of Production:** Aliza Greenblatt
**Manufacturing Buyer:** Dave Dickey
**Production Coordinator:** Ken Liao
**Marketing Manager:** Richard Seltzer

**McClanahan & Company, Inc.**
**Editorial, Design, Production and Packaging**
**Project Director:** Susan Cornell Poskanzer
**Creative Director:** Lisa Olsson
**Design Director:** Toby Carson
**Director of Production:** Karen Pekarne

© 1996 by Prentice Hall Regents
Prentice Hall, Inc.
A Viacom Company
Upper Saddle River, NJ 07458

PRENTICE HALL REGENTS
A VIACOM COMPANY

Printed in the United States of America

10  9  8  7  6  5  4  3  2

ISBN 0-13-349879-4

Prentice-Hall International (UK) Limited, London
Prentice-Hall of Australia Pty. Limited, Sydney
Prentice-Hall Canada Inc., Toronto
Prentice-Hall Hispanoamerican, SA., Mexico
Prentice-Hall of India Private Limited, New Delhi
Prentice-Hall of Japan, Inc., Tokyo
Simon & Schuster Asia Pte. Ltd., Singapore
Editora Prentice-Hall do Brasil, Ltda., Rio de Janeiro

**Acknowledgments**
*Grateful acknowledgment is made to the following publishers, authors, and agents for their permission to reprint copyrighted material. The following literature appears in both Teacher's and Student Books:*

**Thomas Y. Crowell Junior Books:** *What Happened to the Dinosaurs?* by Franklyn M. Branley. Text copyright © 1989 by Franklyn M. Branley. Illustrations copyright © 1989 by Marc Simont. Reprinted by permission of HarperCollins Publishers.

**Cover**
Jeff Shelly

**Photo Credits**
Michael Dick/Animals, Animals p18; Ken Karp Photography p17, p22; Bruce Selyem/Museum of the Rockies/Montana State University p19

**Art Credits**
Alex Bloch p10–11; Daniel Del Valle p19 (top right), p22; Kate Flanagan p17; Steve Flanagan p23; Bart Goldman p21; Vinton Lennon p20; Paul Meinel p18 (top right), Julie Pace p18 (bottom center, center right), p19 (bottom); Gregg Whitlock p2–3; Toby Williams p4–8; Ron Zalme p9, p20